GREAT LIVES

THIS BOOK BELONGS TO

The books listed below have been referred to in the writing of this book, with the permission of the author, Ruskin Bond.

Rain in the Mountains: Notes from the Himalayas (Penguin)

Scenes from a Writer's Life (Penguin)

The Lamp is Lit: Leaves from a Journal (Penguin)

Notes from a Small Room (Penguin)

Landour Days: A Writer's Journal (Penguin)

Ruskin, Our Enduring Bond (Roli Books)

The India I Love (Rupa)

Love Among the Bookshelves (Penguin/Viking)

A Town Called Dehra (Penguin)

The Very Best of Ruskin Bond (Rupa)

Published by Scholastic India Pvt. Ltd.
A subsidiary of Scholastic Inc., New York, 10012 (USA).
Publishers since 1920, with international operations in Canada,
Australia, New Zealand, the United Kingdom, India, and Hong Kong.

For information regarding permission, write to:
Scholastic India Pvt. Ltd.
A-27, Ground Floor, Sigma Centre
Infocity-1, Sector 34, Gurgaon 122001 (India)

This edition: December 2016

This Reprint edition: March 2025

ISBN-13: 978-93-8631-370-6

Printed at Shiv Shakti Printing & Trading Co., Haryana

RUSKIN BOND

Text: Shamim Padamsee
Art: Rayika Sen

SCHOLASTIC
New York Toronto London Auckland
Sydney New Delhi Hong Kong

SHAMIM PADAMSEE loves discovering India—its peoples, cultures, flora, fauna, arts, crafts and amazing diversity. She is happiest when she is researching and writing. She has 11 book titles to her name so far. These include *Great Lives: A. P. J. Abdul Kalam* and *Little Flamingo Searches for Food* (both Scholastic India); *A Silly Story of Bondapalli, Carry Me, Mama, Watch Out!, The Great Birdywood Games, Birdywood Buzz* and *Dancing on Walls* (all Tulika); *Adventures of the Magic Jharoka: Rebels in Rajasthan* and *Adventures of the Magic Jharoka: Poachers in Paradise* (both Puffin) and *Scarecrows on Parade* (Pratham Books).

She runs a website called Young India Books and the Leading Reading Schools of India Award programme.

RAYIKA SEN is a visual communication designer with a passion for illustration! Colours and patterns weave her illustrations and her characters are her favourite subjects. A graduate of Srishti School of Art, Design and Technology, Bangalore, Rayika has worked for publishers, toy-makers, design studios and her illustrations have been featured in international platforms like AFCC, Singapore. Her doodles and snippets can be seen on her facebook page: Rayeeeka (www.facebook.com/rayeeeka) or her website (rayika.weebly.com)!

Foreword

Being an old-fashioned, lazy sort of fellow, I should really be writing a Backword instead of a Foreword, and it ought to appear at the end of this book instead of at the beginning.

As the author of many books, it's nice to have someone else doing all the writing, making me the subject of a colourful graphic biography, full of kind words and lively pictures. It makes me feel like a comic book hero!

But I'm no hero. I have more in common with a spider than with Spiderman; more affinity with a bat than with Batman. Like a spider, I sit quietly on a wall and wait for stories (rather than insects) to come to me. And like a bat, I have been known to roam about in the night—again, looking for stories.

I have been doing this for over sixty-five years, and my story cupboard is overflowing.

I now pass the baton on to the many talented young writers who are the storytellers of tomorrow.

And I hope this story of my writing life—told so lovingly by Shamim Padamsee and wonderfully illustrated by Rayika Sen—will help others on the way to becoming good readers, good writers, good people.

Ruskin Bond
Landour, Mussoorie
January, 2017

GREAT LIVES

With a unique mix of text and the comic book format, the **SCHOLASTIC BIOGRAPHIES SERIES** captures the '**GREAT LIVES**' that have inspired generations and continue to motivate young and old alike.

CHAPTER 1

Now, Now, Brown Cow

Trrr-ing! The alarm bell rang. And even before the last trrr-ing could go off, the young man had already jumped out of bed and flung open the window of his room located on the first floor of Bibiji's house. Cold air rushed in. He shivered slightly, wrapped his arms across his chest and stuck his head out. The sky was beginning to transform from a deep indigo to a dark blue. Towards the east, a flush of pale pink and gold was starting to spread across the horizon.

A flock of snowy white egrets winged their way across the sky. He cheerfully waved to them. "Have a great day!" he called out. From the leafy branches of a litchi tree, a red-vented bulbul struck up a melody to welcome the dawn. From a nearby mango tree, parakeets, barbets and other birds joined in and soon a merry little band was heralding the arrival of this much-awaited day. Finally, the sun peeped out of the horizon. He dashed down the stairs eagerly, two at a time, and sprinted down the dusty road. A cold breeze was blowing, but he did not feel it as he was warmed by the thought of seeing his first work in print.

The road was deserted at this time of the day, except for a solitary milkman trundling down the road carefully, balancing two large cans of milk suspended on each end of a long pole. Finally, he turned the corner and spotted the newsagent seated on the ground sorting the piles of newspapers that had just arrived via the Dehradun Express.

"Has the *Illustrated Weekly* come in?" he asked him anxiously.
"Yes, it has. Why do you ask?"
"My story should be in there," replied the young man, excitedly rubbing his hands together.
"Ah-ha, that's good news! Will it help increase my circulation?" asked the agent in a matter-of-fact tone, as he pointed to the pile of partially hidden magazines.
"Perhaps," the young man responded, and unable to restrain himself any further, he reached out for the copy that lay tantalisingly in front of him. His hands were trembling but it had nothing to do with the cold morning air. He quickly flipped through it and finally, towards the end of the magazine, he spotted it. Blazing across the page was the heading, *The Room on the Roof* – Part One, by Ruskin Bond.

He pointed it out to the newsagent with a smile that almost stretched from ear to ear, and said, "I'll take one of these. No wait! Make that three copies," he added, feeling generous, although he knew that the cost of the additional copies would dip into his meagre funds.
"Well, sure is my lucky day today," said the agent, grinning cheekily. "My circulation has already gone up!"

Ruskin Bond tucked the magazines under his arm and walked back up the road. He felt on top of the world. His story was in print! The sky looked bluer, the air smelled sweeter and the birdsongs—a symphony orchestra. He opened the magazine and looked at it again. He felt like shouting from the rooftops to let the world know that he had finally arrived; that he was now a published author...but he had no one to share his good news with. His beloved father had passed away many years ago. His mother and stepfather had moved to Delhi and he had no mentor or teacher who would say to him, "Shabaash. Well done, Bond!"

Feeling a bit forlorn and lonely and in a somewhat pensive mood, he walked down the road and spotted a cow silently chewing cud in the middle of the road.

Why hello, Mrs Cow!
A very good morning to you!
MOO-OO
Guess what? I am now a published author! Look here. It says, *The Room on the Roof* by Ruskin Bond.
THE ROOM ON THE ROOF
MOO-OO-OOO
Why, thank you for your good wishes.
ROOM ON THE
Oh-no-no, you silly cow!
That is not what it's meant for!

Relieved that he could save his precious treasure from becoming a meal for the greedy cow, he turned around and briskly walked back to his little room on the first floor of Bibiji's house, opened the magazine and re-read the story that he had already read a million times before (at least it felt like that). However, this time it was different. It was not a manuscript any longer. It was in print!

After he had finished reading it, he closed his eyes and sank into a deep reverie, and his life thus far flashed before his eyes.

CHAPTER 2

Early Days

Ruskin Owen Bond was born on May 19, 1934 in the military hospital in Kasauli, Himachal Pradesh, a small town nestled in the foothills of the Himalayas.

However, he did not live there for long. When he was just a couple of years old, the Jam Saheb—ruler of the princely state of Jamnagar—appointed his father as tutor to the royal princesses. The family had to relocate from the cool climate of the hill-station to the warm sandy shores of the Arabian Sea.

Bond's earliest memories of his childhood are those of walking on pristine beaches, digging his toes into the cool sand and picking up shells. Sometimes he would put one to his ear and imagine that the sound of the sea was magically trapped inside.

"Oh, I wish I could go there too," said Little Ruskin, imagining himself sailing away in swift-moving ships to these exotic-sounding places, having great adventures, perhaps meeting a pirate or two, although he generally preferred having his feet firmly planted on *terra firma.*

During their stay in Jamnagar, Bond and his family lived in the humongous palace grounds. There never was a dull moment for him as there was so much to do and so many exciting nooks and crannies to explore and discover. One day, he discovered a huge patch of flowering cosmos plants—with white, purple and pink blossoms. The plants towered over his head. He wandered through his own little flowering forest, watching them toss their pretty heads happily in the breeze.

Another time, he found an old disused well in the corner of a garden. Countless pigeons had decided to make their home in it. Bond would sit there for hours on end and listen to their complaints—it's a guttur-guttur day, some would say, and the others would move the brilliant blue-green feathers of their necks forward and back and moan, "Yes, for sure, yes, for sure."

On hot summer days, it was the turn of the brainfever birds (hawk-cuckoo) to complain, "How hot it's getting!" and then all the others would chorus loudly in an ever-rising crescendo, "We feel it! We feel it! WE FEEL IT!"

Once, whilst exploring another part of the garden, he spotted a snake. When the snake became aware of his presence, it quickly slithered away into the bushes. Ruskin was fascinated by the S-shaped, wavy motion of the snake. When he got back home, he tried to creep on his belly just like the snake.

"What are you doing, Ruskin?" asked his mother. "Watch, Mummy, I'm a snake!" said Ruskin. But, he soon got tired of creeping on the ground after realising that it was not as simple as it looked. He decided that being able to walk was a far better way of moving around.

However, his most exciting discovery was that of the old deserted palace. It was grand, with tall turrets and thick walls. He peeped inside through one of the windows and spotted dark mysterious passages. His curiosity aroused, Bond snooped around, trying to find a way to get in. And then, he spotted an elaborately decorated spiral staircase rising all the way to the sky, or so it seemed to him. Just as Jack could not resist climbing the beanstalk that had sprung up near his window, so also little Ruskin could not resist the temptation of trying to discover what wondrous worlds lay above. He began to climb. Round and round the staircase twisted and turned—this way and that. Finally, he reached a small platform with an elaborately carved door. He pushed the door. It opened slowly. Bond stepped inside. It was a little room. He looked around. It was magical! Every wall had big beautiful stained-glass windows—each one a different colour. Excited, he ran from one to another. As he peered through them, the world turned either green or red or blue or yellow. He was entranced. Many years later, he wrote a story woven around it, titled, 'The Room of Many Colours'.

During their time in Jamnagar, Bond and his family—mother, father and his handicapped sister, Ellen, lived in three different homes. The first one, Cambridge House, was a rambling old colonial mansion that leaked every monsoon: during every downpour they had to run around and place pots and pans all over the room to catch the drips. Another house, a wing of the old palace, the Lal Baug, housed some exciting tenants—bats and cobras! Lastly, they moved into the Tennis Bungalow, a large airy building that used to house a sports pavilion, located in the grounds of the Ram Vilas Palace.

Sometimes, his father would take him to the schoolroom that was set up in one of the palace bungalows. It was attended by the three princesses, who were usually dressed in bandhgala jackets and trousers. At first, Bond thought that they were boys and was annoyed when one of them kept pinching his rosy cheeks and hugging him. But when he discovered that she was a princess, he was quite happy. However, he was generally shy of the boyish princesses and remained shy of girls right until his teens.

Bond enjoyed hanging around the classroom and observing the class in progress. As he had already learnt to read, he would stand close by and peer at the books from above. Soon, he was quite adept at reading books upside down. He still does that sometimes, just for fun.

But those idyllic days in Jamnagar soon came to an end. Dark clouds were looming not just over the world because of the impending Second World War, but also in his own little life. His world was going to change dramatically, and definitely not for the better.

CHAPTER 3

Wars and Woes

It was the year 1941. The world was engulfed in the most devastating war in history—the Second World War. Nations of the world were divided into two camps—the Axis powers and the Allies. They fought bitterly against each other—on land, in the skies and in the seas, resulting in large-scale suffering and destruction everywhere.

As England was in the thick of the war, Bond's father patriotically decided to do his bit for his country and joined the Royal Air Force (RAF). He was appointed pilot officer, although his real job was to cipher and decipher codes in the Intelligence department located in Delhi.

War clouds were also looming within Bond's family. He could sense that all was not well between his parents. They were bickering all the time and often his mother would go away for days on end by herself.

Soon, the family left Jamnagar and relocated to Dehradun. For some reason his parents decided that Bond would be better off in a boarding school and he was admitted to a convent school in Mussoorie.

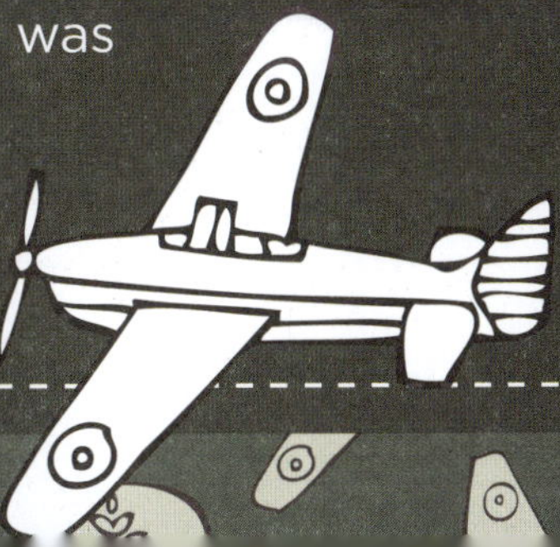

This particular boarding school was no fun at all. Bond was miserable there. The nuns were strict and unsympathetic, the food was terrible (stringy meat boiled with pumpkin) and the students unfriendly. He often thought of running away, but where could he run to? He wrote many pleading letters to his parents to take him out of school, but who pays heed to a little boy's woes?

So, one day, when his mother suddenly turned up in the middle of the school year, and told him, "Pack up your things, Ruskin, you are leaving school," his heart leapt with joy. Her words sounded like music to his ears. Delighted, he ran to the dormitory to gather his belongings. Finally! he thought. All his pleading had convinced his parents to take him out of the school.

The taxi was loaded, goodbyes were said and they were off. The road twisted and turned and plunged down the steep slopes. As they descended towards the plains, the tall pine and deodar of the mountains gave way to the sal, sheesham and ficus trees. Gradually the trees became fewer and the air warmer. They had reached Dehra.

But to Bond's surprise, instead of turning off towards his grandmother's house, they headed towards the railway station.

"Where are we going, Mummy?"
"You are going to meet your father, in Delhi," she said.
"With you?"
"No. You are going alone."
"B...but... why, Mummy?"
"You will not understand, child."
Looking at his crestfallen face, his mother said, "Don't worry, Ruskin, Daddy will be there at the station to receive you."
And that was the end of the conversation.

They sat on the bench in silence. Bond was puzzled. Something did not feel right. Soon, he heard the sound of the approaching train...thud, thud, thud. Louder and louder, resonating with the ominous thudding in his little heart. Finally, the green and gold train appeared in a burst of fiery embers and smoke, and it was time to board.

Mother helped him carry his suitcase, his bedding roll and a canteen of water onto the train. A shrill whistle blew. The train was about to depart. "Goodbye Ruskin," said mother, and giving him a peck on his cheek, she stepped off the train.

Early next morning, the steam engine huffed and puffed into Delhi station accompanied by the sound of clanging bells, shrill whistles and the cacophony of hustling coolies and bustling families. Bond spotted his father, waiting for him on the platform, looking very handsome in his military khakis and blue RAF cap. All his misgivings vanished.

"Daddy!" he shouted. And hopping off the train, he smartly saluted his father, only to be swept up in his loving arms.

Uncle Fred, the station superintendent at Delhi railway station, was also there with his father.
"You must be starving, young man. Come along, let's all go have a cuppa at my house."

Uncle Fred's sprawling bungalow was not far from the station. In those days there were very few cars, and people usually travelled by tonga, a simple horse-driven carriage. Bond hopped in beside the hefty mustachioed tonga-wallah. A tug on the reins and a light flick of the whip and the pony took off, his hooves clip-clopping on the dusty mud roads.

Soon they were at the bungalow. As they disembarked, there was a round of saluting by the staff and they were whisked off to the dining room where the cook had laid out a lavish breakfast. There was fresh bread, butter, several kinds of jam and an assortment of biscuits. So many months of unappetising food plus the long train journey had contributed to a few loud rumbles in his stomach.

Father was telling Uncle Fred that he and his wife had separated.
Oh dear, that is awful. What happened?
Don't exactly know. Perhaps she did not like my sedate lifestyle. You see, she is far younger than me and likes to live it up...parties and such, you know.
Is there someone else?
Yes. She has got involved with an Indian gentleman, Hari. He owns a motor garage in Dehra.
Damn! What are you doing about the kids?
Well, Ellen will have to go to my mother in Calcutta, Ruskin will stay with me. And, as William is still a baby, he will continue to be with her.
Bond was all shaken up. His little world was coming apart. His family was going to be scattered. However, the only ray of sunshine was that he would be staying with his father whom he adored with all his little heart.

He walked up to his father and quietly slipped his little hand into his strong big one. Father squeezed it a bit and wrapped his arm around him. Bond felt reassured. As long as he had his father by his side, he was confident that everything would be alright.

CHAPTER 4

Daddy's Little Boy

In spite of everything, this was one of the happiest years in little Ruskin's life. The World War was in full swing, but as it was being fought in distant places, such as Europe, Burma and the Far East, it did not affect most people in India. The marital discord between his parents, too, seemed far away.

Besides, there was a lot to do in Delhi—movies to see, places to eat at, monuments to discover and best of all, no school! In short, life was perfect.

When he had first arrived in Delhi, his father was living in a tent situated on a hot, dusty plain. As the hot dry winds swept across the plains, swirls of dust would rise from the parched earth, like mini-tornados. To stay, if not cool, at least comfortable, father hung a khas-khas reed mat over the door. Every hour a bhisti would come along with his goat-skin bag slung over one shoulder and drench it with water. Immediately, the temperature inside the tent would come down by several degrees and a sweet fragrance would permeate the air.

Soon after his arrival, they moved 'house' to a hutment near Humayun's tomb. Bond enjoyed the long evening walks with his little hand tucked into his father's, as they explored the old crumbling tombs and monuments inhabited by an array of wildlife—blackbuck and nilgai; mongoose and snakes; monitor lizards and chameleons; song birds and water birds.

The next move was to Atul Grove Road, then to a small flat on Hailey Road, and finally to an apartment in Scindia House, facing Connaught Circus.

Of all the homes he had lived in, Bond loved being in the heart of the city, with myriads of shops, restaurants, book shops, record shops and, best of all, cinema houses! His father was a movie buff and together they would visit the theatres as often as they could. In fact, Bond regularly maintained a diary listing not only the names of all the movies they saw, but also the cast of the films and other details.

When they were not watching movies, they listened to music on his father's old gramophone.
"Will you wind up the gramophone, Rus...?" Before father could even finish his sentence, Bond would have leapt out of his couch, energetically cranked the handle, placed the record on the turntable and lowered the needle onto it.

Listening to music then was not as simple as it is in today's day and age of iPods and other devices. One had to make sure that the gramophone was wound up properly, the needle was changed after every use, and that the records were stored flat, otherwise they would get all wonky with the heat.

They listened to all kinds of music—opera, folk, ballad and lighter pop songs. Often, they would go to a record store and browse through the shelves before picking a couple to add to father's already huge collection.

At other times, they would pore over father's extensive stamp collection—two trunks full! Father knew all about his precious stamps and had an album for each country.
As they pored over the collection, Bond learnt history, geography and even biology.
Why are there butterflies on all these stamps, Daddy?
9 BRITISH SOLOMON
BRITISH SOLOMON
3 BRITISH SOLOMON
Because, the Solomon Islands are famous for their butterflies.
Oh look, Daddy, what a funny hat that man is wearing!
ZANZIBAR
6 4
That man is the Sultan of Zanzibar and that funny hat, as you call it, is a fez cap.
Daddy, are there any zebras in India?
KENYA
No, zebras are only found in a few African countries—Kenya, Tanganyika and Uganda.

And so on it went. He learnt that the Pitcairn Islands was inhabited largely by mutineers from the *HMS Bounty*. And that the handsome young hero on Greek stamps was Achilles, a Greek god with a sore heel.

One day, an American officer dropped in for dinner. After the meal, they pored over father's stamp collection. The man picked out several, and to Bond's surprise, paid a couple of thousand rupees for them!

That incident taught Bond that it was possible to make money even from one's hobby. A lesson he remembered when writing became his passion.

However, although his father went out of his way to keep little Ruskin happy, all was not well with his own health. He kept having repeated attacks of malaria—a disease difficult to treat in those days—and often had to be hospitalised. But Bond was not unduly worried. His father always bounced back to health.

However, father decided that it was time for him to go back to school. Perhaps, it was partly due to his indifferent health and partly because he felt that his son needed to be in a formal school structure.

"It's high time you get back to school, young man," said father one day.
"W...hy? I don't need school," wailed Bond, unhappy at the thought of leaving his father. "I can read and I can write. I can even do sums!"

"Yes, my boy, you are quite good for an eight-year-old. But you still need to learn algebra, physics and chemistry."
"No, I don't."
"Oh yes, you do. How else will you earn a living?"
"I have decided to be a tap dancer when I grow up."
"Young man, you have been watching too many movies. It's all my fault. I am now even more convinced that it is best that you go to a boarding school."

Bond was on slippery ground here. Sensing that the argument was not going in his favour, he quickly changed his tactic. "B...but, who will look after you, Daddy? You'll be very lonely."

"You're right. I will be heartbroken after you leave, but it can't be helped," said father, smiling. "I guess I'll have to learn to manage on my own. Besides, I am most probably being posted to Karachi and will not be allowed to keep you with me anyway."
"Oh Daddy, please, please, please don't send me away."

"Don't worry, my boy. I have found a very nice school for you in Shimla. You will love it there. And it is only for a few years. Once the war is over we will both be heading out to England."

Bond realised that his father's mind was made up and nothing would change it. He resigned himself to what he thought would be another bad experience. However, he was in for a happy surprise.

CHAPTER 5

School is Cool

It was the summer of 1943. Bond and his father took the quaint little toy train to Shimla. The train huffed and puffed up the steep mountain slopes, and let out a shrill whistle every time it plunged through long dark tunnels—103 of them!

Eager to look at every bit of the landscape rushing by, Bond stuck his face out of the window. The train happened to be moving across an especially sharp bend. "Daddy, Daddy, I can see the whole train!" he shouted excitedly.
Suddenly, the steam engine belched out a black cloud of soot. Poor Bond! His face and clothes became black and grimy. "You look like a chimney sweep, Ruskin!" his father laughed.

They reached Shimla at lunchtime and dined at Davico's, a restaurant famous for its meringues. Bond popped one into his mouth. At first crunch, the meringue melted in his mouth. "Yumm!" he said, and quickly gobbled up the entire plateful to the amusement of his father.

The next day, they set off for Chhota Shimla, where the Bishop Cotton Prep School was located. The school was known as 'The Eton of the East'. It was an imposing structure, with a lofty motto—'Treat Evil with Good'—and had adopted all the British traditions of public schools in England—such as ragging, and flogging, compulsory games and larger-than-life prefects.

As they approached the school, he spotted the playground where the boys were at recess. Some were spinning tops whilst others were wrestling or jostling each other or playing catch. One was chasing butterflies with a net. He spied a couple of them huddled in a corner, reading comic books. So far, so good.

Instead, it looked at them disdainfully, giving them a baleful eye, and continued to sit on the bald head as though it was the most natural thing in the world. Bond later discovered that the man was a teacher called Mister Jones and the pigeon was his pet.

He was an unusual man with unusual habits; dressed in an unusual style and with unusual convictions. He refused to dole out corporal punishment to the boys—caning, slapping and whacking the kids, as was the norm in those days. The staff looked upon him as an oddball, whilst, on the other hand, the students looked upon him as a great teacher, mentor and confidante.

All in all, the students here seemed to be much happier than those in his previous school. Bond heaved a sigh of relief. Perhaps boarding school was not such a bad idea, after all.

And soon he was a part of it. The school schedule was pretty hectic and regimented. It aimed to give children exposure to a wide range of subjects. Participating in all sports was compulsory. Bond found most games rather boring, especially cricket. He did not see any sense in bowling endless overs to an important player who was practicing his shots; even much less, waiting for a chance to bat and then be given out by the umpire. Bond quickly hit upon a very valid excuse—a cramp in his leg—and thus was excused from playing for the rest of the session. He would happily head straight for the dormitory where he would snuggle in his blanket and enjoy an hour or two of undisturbed sleep.

Bond was not the sporty type. However, he was a good athlete, and excelled as a goalkeeper both in hockey and in football. He was an important member of his school team and played in inter-school competitions against Lawrence School, Sanawar, and others. He made spectacular saves for his team that often resulted in his school walking away with the trophy.

A few years later, when he was older, Bond, who was also good at shot-put, accidently dropped the shot right on to the foot of his coach. The coach hollered a big ear-splitting "Yeowww!"

Since this was an accident, the teacher could not punish him, but he sneakily did the next best thing. When it was Bond's turn in the boxing ring, to get his revenge, he placed him against a very seasoned player. One look at his opponent made Bond decide that it was far better to end the match in the very first round instead of getting beaten and battered over a couple. And so, he head-butted his hapless opponent like an angry bull and was promptly disqualified. He was safe. Hurray!

Besides sports, there were excursions and scouting camps in which the students had to show off their prowess in various areas such as setting up tents, rock-climbing and trekking. Bond, sadly, had not earned a single badge so far, and so one day, when he found one lying on the ground, he quickly pinned it onto his sleeve. Unfortunately for him, it was for achieving merit in cooking. The unsuspecting teacher assigned him the task of cooking for the very hungry scouters. And as you can imagine, the results were disastrous.

In the dormitory at night after lights out, there was even more fun to be had. Pillows would be hurled at each other with whoops of delight and sometimes murderous joy in pummeling someone with whom one wanted to get even. Sometimes the pillows would burst open and the feathers would rise up in the air as in a snowstorm, much to the delight of the students. Unfortunately, one day the headmaster's wife heard the commotion and went to find out what was causing it. As she walked in, a pillow landed on her and burst open. Taken by surprise, she slid down on the ground. The dorm reverberated with uncontrollable laughter. Needless to say, they all got a good spanking on their butts with her extra large hairbrush!

However, the best part of school was the library. Bond's housemaster, realising his passion for reading, placed him in charge of the Anderson Library. Bond now had access to the keys and his joy knew no bounds. It was like receiving the secret password to Aladdin's treasure trove. Often he would take a book to his dormitory and after lights out, pull out his pocket torch, slip under the blanket and read on until sleep took over and he drifted into a wonderful land of dreams inhabited by all his favourite characters—Tom Sawyer, Gulliver, Long John Silver, the Mad Hatter, Sinbad, Cinderella, Ariel and others.

CHAPTER 6

Remember this Day

School life was all-engulfing. They had to rise early and their days were filled with endless rounds of classes, games, homework and dormitory inspections. Breaking the monotony were scout camps at Tara Devi and picnics at the Brockhurst tennis courts. Unlike his previous school, the food was good. Although on account of the war, there was a rationing of food, and breakfast generally comprised of omelettes made from dehydrated egg powder, he had to admit that they were actually quite decent. Lunch was usually curry and rice and for dinner they were served cutlets or chops.

The months flew by. Bond had settled into the school routine and made some great friends. He was full of fun and very popular with the students. He often took the lead in many things, including playing pranks. The students had nicknames for each other and Bond was nicknamed Bulletman by his friends—after one of the popular comic book characters of those times. As the World War was still raging, flying heroes were the flavour of the day. Bond's favourites were the Biggles comic books which had a daredevil pilot as hero. Another favourite was Rockfist Rogan of the RAF, who, whenever he was shot down in enemy territory, always got the better of his enemy. He fought the Nazis and then cleverly escaped in one of their own aircraft.

And having a father in the RAF had also made Bond a hero of sorts. All the boys were in awe of him. "Does your father fly bombers or fighter planes?" they asked him. "Both," Bond glibly lied, for he felt that there was not much glamour in codes and ciphers, although they were just as important.

And yet, in spite of the busy schedules and rounds of activities, Bond missed his father and was overjoyed when he received a letter informing him that he would be coming to Shimla during the midsummer break.

He counted the days for his father to arrive. Sadly, father could only get a couple of days' leave and most of it was used up in travelling from distant Calcutta. "I will only be able to spend a day with you," he wrote. "But don't worry, we will make the most of it."

On the day his father was to arrive, Bond impatiently kept looking out for him.

Finally, he spotted him entering the gate. He ran all the way to greet him. Father had recently been promoted to Flight Lieutenant and was dressed in a dark blue RAF uniform and wore his new stripes on his chest. Bond's little heart filled with pride!

His father held him up and swung him around. “Whoa! How tall you’ve grown in these last few months. Soon I will not be able to carry you, my boy.” Bond’s cup of happiness was overflowing.

“So, how shall we spend the day? Where do you want to go first?” asked father.
“Davico’s!” Bond responded without a moment’s hesitation. It was a favourite of all the eternally hungry school boys. Bond loved the curry puffs, meringues, marzipans and the whole array of pastries being sold there.

He stuffed himself with the goodies, and also took some along just in case he got hungry again. Father and son set off for a walk up a steep hill to ‘deodar-crowned Jakko, shouldering the stars,’ in Kipling’s words. There they visited the Jakhu temple, also called the monkey temple. Seeing the goodies in Bond’s hands, the monkeys decided that they needed them far more than Bond. They snatched the bag from his startled hands and quickly scampered up a tree with their loot and had a feast.

They returned to the Mall and took a rickshaw pulled by four sturdy rickshaw-pullers.
Did you know that Rudyard Kipling had lived in Shimla for many years and some of his stories are set here?
Bond had not yet read books by Kipling, but was fascinated to know that many of his stories were set in Shimla, including a ghost story!
CURIOSITY SHOP
ANTIQUES
Do you see that tiny shop? That is where the boy Kim got his training as a spy from the mysterious Lurgan Sahib, in the story titled *Kim*.
Tell me the ghost story, father, he pleaded.

As the wheels of the rickshaw clattered over the cobbled roads around Elysium Hill father narrated the story of 'The Phantom Rickshaw' about a love affair gone sour. In the end the lady died of a broken heart but she got her revenge by haunting her ex-lover. The story sent a shiver down little Bond's spine and aroused hunger pangs.

"Time to eat again?" asked father, smiling down at his little boy.

Lunch over, they headed to the theatre for the movies. Bond's father was very fond of the movies. During the year that they were in Delhi, they must have seen at least 30 films together. Bond, too, had become very fond of the cinema and kept notes in his diary of all the films he saw; who produced the film, who the actors were; and could rattle off the names of all the yesteryear stars.

That night they stayed on Elysium Hill. The next day, before heading back to school, they went for a long walk to Kasumpti, ate a picnic lunch and as they walked back, father talked about the forthcoming winter vacation. "Calcutta Granny and Ellen are looking forward to seeing you."
Bond nodded happily, excited at the thought of seeing his sister again.
"You will love Calcutta, my boy. There are bookshops and cinemas and Chinese restaurants. There are also good gramophone shops from where we can buy records. What fun we will have!"

They had reached the school gate. It was time to part. "Remember this day, Ruskin," father said, and after one last hug, he slowly walked away. Bond's eyes lingered on him until he was a mere speck.

That was the very last time he saw his father.

CHAPTER 7

Why, God, why?

Ruskin Bond's grandfather had arrived in India in the 1880s, after joining the Scottish Rifles regiment as a foot soldier. His grandmother, Gloriana, was an orphan. She had grown up on an indigo plant in Bihar.

Being foot soldiers meant that the regiment was constantly being moved from one place to another. Bond's father, Aubrey Alexander Bond, was born in a small town called Shahjahanpur, which coincidentally became the setting for his novella, *A Flight of Pigeons*.

After retirement, Grandfather settled down in Calcutta, where he died. He was a quiet reclusive kind of person who never lost his temper with anyone. His favourite pastime? Watching jugglers and street acrobats! Bond's grandmother continued to live in Calcutta and was referred to as Calcutta Granny.

Because of his father's army background, Aubrey Alexander studied in the Lawrence Royal Military School at Sanawar. After finishing his schooling, he signed up for a teachers' training course in Lovedale, Ooty. It was there that he met Bond's mother—Edith.

His first teaching job was on the invitation of the Maharaja of Alwar. There he taught the members of the royal household. A couple of years later he was invited by the Jam Saheb of the princely state of Jamnagar (Nawanagar) to teach the royal princesses.

By then, Aubrey Alexander was married and had had two children, Ruskin and Ellen. Bond was a little more than a year old at that time. Packing bag and baggage, the family moved to Kathiawar.

Father was very good-looking and yet a gentle and caring person. More importantly, he was a great father who guided his son with love and understanding. Bond remembers his father reading *Alice in Wonderland* and *Peter Pan* to him and also teaching him how to read and write.

The two of them shared a warm and loving relationship. After returning home from work, his father would spend a lot of time with him, and later, when he joined boarding school, he would regularly send him greeting cards and write long letters. Bond adored his dad.

One day, Mr Murtough, his school teacher said, "Come walk with me, Ruskin, there is something important I want to talk to you about." Bond felt a sense of foreboding. It was not common for teachers to ask students to accompany them on walks. His heart lurched. He stepped out into the playground with his teacher and just as he had feared, it was bad news.

Unsure of how to break the news to the vulnerable little boy, the teacher mumbled, "God needed your father with him in heaven and so has taken him."

The sky seemed to collapse on Bond's head. He started to tremble all over.
Unaware of what the boy beside him was feeling, the uncaring teacher just wanted to get his task over and done with, and continued, "The frequent bouts of malaria had weakened his body, as a result of which he could not withstand the severe attack of jaundice..."

Bond had stopped listening. Why, God, why? he shrieked silently. How can you need my father more than I do? You have everything. I only had him. How could you take him away, God? Tell me! Why? Why?

He felt sick and nearly passed out. The teacher took him to the infirmary where he spent a couple of days. Memories of his father flooded his being.

He remembered the first time his father had taken him to watch a train. Hand in hand, they stood on a bridge. In front of them was a dark tunnel. At first, he heard a shrill whistle and then with a roar that made the bridge tremble, the train emerged from the tunnel—a green and gold monster snorting fire in a dark cave. Petrified, little Bond ran into his father's protective arms, shouting, "Dragon! Dragon!"

He remembered the time his father had brought him a small diary and encouraged him to write in it regularly, perhaps laying the foundation for his future career in writing.

He remembered his father's passion for stamp collection. How he would open the large tin trunks in which they were stored and how they would pore over them together and get transported to far-off places—Greece, Newfoundland, Borneo, Zanzibar and others.

He remembered the innumerable movies that they watched together and how they laughed and discussed them over a milkshake.

He remembered the walks amongst the ruins of Delhi, discovering interesting nooks and crannies.

He remembered the humorous postcards his father would regularly send him. His favourite was part of a series of an ape-like character called Granpop. One showed Granpop doing the rumba in the rain. "Is this how you feel now that the rains are here?" father had written.

He remembered how his heart filled with pride whenever he saw his father, fully dressed in his Royal Air Force (RAF) uniform. And how he would smartly salute him before being swept into his loving arms.

Why, God, why? He sobbed silently. He felt alone, all alone. What was to become of him? he wondered. He lay in the infirmary for a couple of days, surrounded by the letters that his beloved father had written to him. He read them over and over again. They were all that he had left of his father.

One day, his housemaster, Mr Priestly, walked into the infirmary, and seeing the letters scattered around him, asked, "Would you like me to keep them for you? I will return them when you go home for your break." Although he did not want to part with his treasure, he could not say no, and so he reluctantly handed them over.

When school was closing for the vacation, he went to the housemaster's office.
"Sir, can I have my letters back?"
"What letters?"
"My father's letters, Sir. You told me to give them to you for safe-keeping."
"Why would I do that?"
Mr Priestly casually opened a few drawers and peeked into them. "I don't see them here," he said nonchalantly. "If I find them, I will give them to you. Now run along, boy. I am very busy."

Bond was stunned. All those precious memories of his father, the only things that he had left of him were gone. Letters filled with the warmth of his love and messages of hope and plans for the future. They had vanished, just like his father. He never saw the letters again, and happily for him, never saw the beastly Mr Priestly again.

All he had left with him was just one letter.

All he had left with him was just one letter.

F/Lt. A.A. Bond 109485. (RAF)
C/o 231 Group,
Rafpost
Calcutta. 20/8/44

My dear Ruskin,

Thank you very much for your letter received a few days ago. I was pleased to hear that you were quite well and learning hard. We are all quite OK. here, but I am still not strong enough to go to work after the recent attack of malaria I had. I was in hospitall for a long time and that is the reason why you did not get a letter from me for several weeks

I have now to wear glasses for reading, but I do not use them for ordinary wear but only when I read or do book work. Ellen does not wear glasses at all now.

Do you need any new warm clothes? Your warm suits must be getting too small. I am glad to hear the rains are practically over in the hills where you are. It will be nice to have sunny days in September when your holidays are on. Do the holiday begin from the 9th of Sept.? What will you do? Is there to be a Scouts Camp at Taradevi? Or will you catch butterflies on sunny days on the School Cricket Ground?

I am glad to hear you have lots of friends. Next year you will be in the top class of the Prep. School. You only have 3½ months more for the Xmas. holidays to come round, then you will be glad to come home I am sure, to do more stamp work and library study. The New Market is full of book shops here. Ellen loves the market.

I wanted to write before about your writing Ruskin, but forgot. Sometimes I get letters from you written in very small handwriting, as if you wanted to squeeze a lot of news into one sheet of letter paper. It is not good for you or for your eyes, to get into the habit of writing too small. I know your handwriting is good & that you came 1st in class for handwriting, but try and form a larger style of writing and do not worry if you can't get all your news into one sheet of paper - but stick to big letters.

We have had a very wet month just passed. It is still cloudy - at night we have to use fans, but during the cold weather it is nice - not too cold like Delhi and not too warm either - but just moderate.

Granny is quite well. She and Ellen send you their fond love. The last time I heard a week ago, that William & Meet Delia were well also.

We have been without a Cook for the past few days. I hope we find a good one before long. There are not many. I wish I could get our Delhi cook, the old man now famous for his "Black Puddings" which Ellen hasn't seen since we arrived in Calcutta 4 months ago.

I have still got all the Records & Gramaphone and most of the best books, but as they are all getting old & some not suited to you, which are only for children under 8 yrs old - I will give some to William & Ellen, and you can buy some new ones when you come home for Xmas. I am re-arranging all the stamps that became loose & topsy-turvy after people came & went through the collections to buy stamps. A good many got sold, the rest got mixed up a bit and it is now taking up all my time putting the balance of the Collection in order. But as I am at home all day, unable to go to work as yet, I have lots of time to finish the work of re-arranging the Collection.

Ellen loves drawing. I give her paper and a pencil and let her draw for herself without any help, to get her used to holding paper & pencil. She has got expert at using her pencil now, and draws some wonderful animals like camels, elephants dragons with many heads - cobras - rain clouds shedding buckets of water - tigers with long grass around them - horses with manes and wolves & foxes with bushy hair. Sometimes you cant see much of the animals because there is too much grass covering them or too much hair on the foxes & wolves and too much mane on the horses necks - or too much rain from the clouds. All this decoration is made up by a sort of heavy scribbling of lines, but through it all one can see some very good shapes of animals elephants & ostriches & other things. I will send you some.

Well Ruskin I hope this finds you well with fond love from us all. Write again soon. Ever Your loving daddy xxxxx

CHAPTER 8

The Homecoming

The winter vacation was drawing near. The school was buzzing with excitement. All that the boys could talk about were their holiday plans with their families; all except Bond. He did not know what was to become of him.

Normally, he would be heading out to his father, but this year he was stuck in no man's land—a wilderness, a dreary landscape—uncharted territories lay in front of him. His teacher had said, God needed your father in heaven and so has taken him. And a little boy was left all alone on earth to fend for himself.

Finally, it was decided that he would be going to Dehra. Even though he had spent many happy years of his childhood there, he was apprehensive. He had not met his mother for a long time, and besides, he would now have to connect with a stepfather whom he had met very briefly; one whom he resented intensely as he believed him to be the cause of the divorce. Dark clouds hovered over his head.

On the last day of school, amidst the excited babble of voices, Bond boarded the train at Dharampur. The train pulled out of the station and slowly gathered momentum. With every clackety-clack of its wheels, it was hurtling him towards a dreaded new phase of his life.

Soon they were in Dehra. There was excitement all around as the boys, part of the Dehra party, were greeted warmly by their families; swung around or hoisted up on shoulders with joy. Hawkers, coolies and families all intermingling in one happy chaos.

Anxiously clutching his small tin trunk, a bedding roll and a hockey stick, Bond hesitatingly stepped off the train. He looked here. He looked there. He could not spot his mother or stepfather anywhere. Slowly, the crowd began to disperse. The station was now almost deserted.

A lone stray dog hung around him hoping to get a tidbit or two. However, as Bond had finished eating his snack in the train, he had nothing to offer him. A disappointed dog and a disappointed boy were soon the only ones left hanging around the station. A sense of panic gripped him. Was he being abandoned? Where was he to go? He did not even have his mother's address.

And then it occurred to him that he would be able to find his way to his grandmother's house. He walked out of the station to a solitary tonga parked outside. He clambered onto the seat next to the tongawalla. "Take me to No 6, Survey Road."

Soon the pony was clip-clopping away on the narrow, dusty paths.

Bond looked around and was happy to see the old familiar landmarks—the rambling bungalows, the old banyan tree, the litchi, guava and mango orchards. Soon he would reach his grandparents' house.

His grandfather, William Dudley, was born in Dera Ismail Khan in the North-West Frontier Province, and had worked for the railways. He was one of the early pioneers who helped bring the railway to Dera. When his grandfather passed away, Ruskin was only about a year old. But all through his childhood, he had heard stories of his wild grandfather who had a love for unusual pets. Inspired by those tales, Bond wrote many fun-filled stories about him and his exotic menagerie. Grandmother Ellen had studied in a school established by the Indian Railways, somewhere between Mussoorie and Dehra. She had finished her schooling at La Martiniere in Lucknow. They had three daughters—Emily, Gwen and Edith. Edith was Ruskin Bond's mother.

They reached their destination. The tonga stopped. Bond jumped off. Granny was in the garden feeding her dog, Crazy, so called because he would run around crazily in circles whenever he saw someone. Crazy immediately recognised Bond, leapt over him, licked him all over and true to his name did a crazy dance around him.

Granny was shocked to see Bond arrive alone. "Didn't anyone meet you at the station?" she asked. Bond shook his head.

Seeing his crumpled face, she said, "Wait here. I'll drop you."

Until she returned, Bond looked around the garden. Memories of happy childhood days flooded his mind. Playing in the garden, climbing the old jackfruit tree, looking at creepy-crawlies and pottering around with Dukhi, the long-faced gardener.

He remembered the time when he had been naughty and was locked in the storeroom by Granny. He had poked around the closet and found a hidden cache of chocolates. Ah, sweet revenge, he thought, and quickly nibbled a bite from each and every one of them. When Granny finally opened the door, and saw the destruction he had caused to her precious chocolates, she let out a blood-curdling scream. Of course, he was punished again, but it was well worth it!

Granny soon emerged from her room and looked at the tonga that Bond had arrived in.
Just my luck that you should arrive in a tonga pulled by a white pony. I hate them.
Why Granny?
Because they are very frisky and are always trying to topple me off.
Just then the pony lifted his tail and let out a big stinky fart right onto their faces—Pheww!
This was followed by huge mounds of dung being plonked in the middle of the road.
Bond burst out laughing and his mood lifted substantially.
But Granny was not at all amused.
See? I told you they are vile creatures!

Soon they had crossed the dry bed of the Rispana river and reached Dalanwala, the area where his mother lived.

They got off the tonga and walked up to the door. It was bolted from the inside. They knocked several times. A servant appeared dressed in a torn shirt and dirty striped pajamas looking decidedly unhappy at being disturbed. He gave Granny a half-hearted salaam.
"Where's the memsahib?" she asked.
"Gone to Motichur for shikar, madam."
"Were they not expecting the boy?"
"They told me that he would be arriving tomorrow, madam."

Suddenly, there was a loud wail. A baby's cry!
"That is your baby brother," Granny told him. "He is six months old."
Bond was stunned. He had no idea that he had a new baby brother.
Granny turned around and headed for the door. "I'm off, Ruskin."
And shaking her head, she walked out, mumbling, "Shikar, indeed! So irresponsible of Edith to take off like that."

That evening his parents returned.
"Hello, Ruskin," said his mother, planting a kiss on his cheeks. "Good to see you again." And then turning around, she called out to the baby's ayah, "How's the baby? Is everything alright?"
"Yes, Madam," came the reply from the baby's room.

Mother then walked to the living room to join his stepfather, who had already settled himself on the couch with his drink. She poured one for herself and sat down beside him.
Bond went to his room. The feeling of abandonment swept over him once again. He climbed onto his bed and buried his face in his pillow. Why, God, why?

CHAPTER 9

F.V.A.D.

(First Vacation After Daddy)

This was the most difficult period in little Bond's life. What he yearned for at that time was to be comforted, to be held, to be loved. Sadly, both his mother and father were so engrossed in their own lives that they did not perceive his sadness. And he was left to cope with it all by himself.

Often Bond wondered why his mother had abandoned his gentle and loving father for Hari. She had been having an affair with the Punjabi businessman even before the divorce had come through. Perhaps Hari, smitten by the vivacious and beautiful young Anglo-Indian girl, must have gone all out to woo her, leaving his wife of many years. She, in turn, was perhaps looking for a change. Maybe her husband, Aubrey Bond, turned out to be a bit too staid for her liking. After all, he was fifteen years her senior. He was generally content with his books, music and stamp collection, whilst she wanted to go out, have fun and party. They were as different as chalk and cheese. Years later, Bond came to terms with it, but, as a young boy, he was scarred. The wounds left by those troubled years stayed with him for a long, long time.

Whilst Hari was not mean or cruel to Bond, he was so wrapped up in himself and his bohemian lifestyle that he was not sensitive to the young boy's needs. He generally ignored the little boy whom he must have felt was thrust upon him—like an unwelcome guest. He was just about ready to tolerate him and no more. You don't get in my way, and I will not get in yours, was his general attitude.

During the war, Dehra was a lively town catering to the war-weary American and British soldiers. It had a recreational centre, cafés, bars and dance halls. Nearby was a camp set up for Italians, part of the Axis alliance, who were captured as prisoners of war. The prevailing mood of the soldiers stationed there was to let their hair down—drink, party, socialise. It gave them a respite from the grim happenings of the war.

His parents, too, were swept away in all the merry-making. They partied as though there were no tomorrow. They would go out almost every night and would return home only in the early hours of the morning. Bond often worried how he would manage in case they had a fatal accident on their way home. Or, in an extreme case, be devoured by a hungry tiger. Did they have savings that would enable him to support himself and his siblings?

He doubted that that was the case. His stepfather, who owned an auto garage, was not a successful businessman by any stretch of the imagination. He always owed money to others. In fact, the family was often forced to move residence, and on one occasion was even thrown out of their home—bag and baggage—on account of rental arrears. Almost every time Bond came home for his vacations, they would be living in a different house! He was lucky that the RAF had undertaken to pay for his schooling and so he could continue to study in Bishop Cotton School.

The strain soon began to tell on their marriage. The two of them separated for some time. Hari returned to his first wife for a short time and his mother took up a job as a manager of Green's Hotel, where Bond was given a room when he went to Dehra for his vacation. But to give her credit, she stuck by his stepfather through thick and thin, even though he was reckless and foolhardy. Life must have been tough for her. She died of cancer at the age of 52.

During those long lonely vacations, Bond dived in even further into the world of books. It was a panacea for his deep sorrow. Whatever he could find to read, he read, as long as it had substance. Once, his stepfather took him for shikar, one of those rare occasions when he acknowledged his presence. However, whilst the hunters went out and shot any animal that moved—big or small—and often without much success, as they were not good shots, Bond preferred to stay back in the dak bungalow where he had discovered a cabinet full of books, and read.

A fifteen-minute walk from home took him to the Ideal Book Store. As he could not afford to buy books, he joined the lending library and for two or three rupees a week he could borrow as many books as he liked! Bond plowed through many of the bestsellers of that time—Betty Smith's *A Tree Grows in Brooklyn*, J. B. Priestly's *The Good Companions*, A. J. Cronin's *The Green Years*, William Saroyan's *The Human Comedy* and practically all the books by P. G. Wodehouse. Bond says that a considerable part of his education came from the Ideal Book Store's lending library.

From the years spent with his father in Delhi, Bond had learnt to love going to the movies. In Dehra, a little road across the maidan took him to the Odeon Cinema. He went there as often as he could to escape from the reality of his home life.

As soon as he got his pocket money, he would head to the theatre, buy the cheapest tickets and settle down and immerse himself in the film. During the interval, they would play music. However, they played the same records over and over again for months on end. Fed up of listening to them,

Bond took 15-20 records from his father's collection at home and gave them to the manager of the Odeon, who was so grateful that he gave Bond a free pass to see as many films as he wanted. All he had to pay was the minuscule amount of entertainment tax. Bond was in seventh heaven!

Dehradun used to be a leafy green town in those days with tea gardens and fields surrounding it. People had hedges surrounding their houses instead of walls. Bond loved exploring the lanes and by-lanes of the town. He often walked towards his grandmother's house. By nature, she was not very forthcoming and not the fun-loving, caring grandmother he has written about in some of his stories (perhaps it was wishful thinking on his part). So he chatted with Dukhi, the old gardener, as he tended his flowers, and also visited Mrs Kellner, a tenant of his grandmother who was severely crippled owing to an unfortunate accident in her early childhood. When she was a baby, a fond uncle had tossed her up in the air and missed catching her, with the result that she fell with a thud to the ground, injured her spine and was handicapped ever since. They struck up a friendship, played card games and board games and before he left, she plied him with cakes and meringues. She was lonely, he was lonely. She loved to feed and he loved to eat. Perfect arrangement!

CHAPTER 10

Tumultuous Times

Slowly, but surely, the vacation drew to a close. It was not as bad as Bond had thought it would be. Mr Hari, his stepfather, generally kept out of his way and Bond was happy to do likewise. It was a stalemate situation: the happy interludes being his visits to the cinema, his on-going passion for books, long walks and the time he spent playing board games with Mrs Kellner. He looked forward to being back in school, though that, too, had its own challenges. This yo-yo of emotions went on right until the time he graduated from school.

The next few years were tumultuous ones—both for Bond and the country.

Lord Mountbatten, the last Viceroy of India, was invited to preside over their Founder's Day event. He spoke to them of the momentous events happening all around the world: the World War was coming to an end; the body of the United Nations was being formulated to ensure peace and harmony on earth, and India's independence was imminent.

The British had agreed to hand over the reins to the Indians. Finally, India's dream of becoming an independent nation was to become a reality. But the country's greatest moment of joy was accompanied by great pain and suffering. The country was partitioned along religious lines. The provinces of Bengal and Punjab were bisected.

This led to the biggest exodus ever, one in which hundreds of thousands of people lost their lives. Hindus leaving their homes, in what was to become Pakistan, and coming to India. Likewise, Muslims leaving theirs and going to Pakistan. Riots broke out. Fires burned. The beastly side of man emerged. Mobs went on a rampage, killing indiscriminately. The canal behind his mother's house was choked with the bodies of riot victims. However, even in the midst of the carnage there were many heart-warming stories of caring people who went out of their way to save their friends—sometimes at great risk to their own lives. Bond's stepfather, too, had his heart in the right place.

He helped many of his Muslim friends escape by driving them to the border in his old Ford convertible. Sadly, the dark shadow of the event soon loomed over the portals of the school. Amidst tears, Muslim children originating in Lahore, Karachi and Peshawar had to bid goodbye. They were to soon board a truck accompanied by an armed escort, leaving behind friends and cherished memories.

Amongst them was Omar, a Muslim boy, Bond's best friend. The story, 'The Playing Fields of Shimla', was inspired by that friendship, which had blossomed on the hockey field. Both of them had played for the School Colts' team. Along the way they had developed a great understanding and were on the same wavelength—a great asset both in their friendship and on the field. They often talked of their personal goals, fears and aspirations.

Once Omar had posed the question of partition to him, "Everyone is saying that our leaders and the British are going to divide the country." And Bond had glibly responded, "Oh, it won't happen. How can they cut up such a big country?" Little did he realise that even whilst they had been talking, the plans for the brutal surgery of the country were well underway—one that was to tear people away from their homes, their loved ones and their friends.

It was now time to bid goodbye to each other.

We will surely meet again someday, Omar.
Inshallah!
And when all the wars are done, a butterfly will still be beautiful.
Oh! That's beautiful. Did you read that somewhere?
Ruskin said no, and Omar smiled.
Already you're a writer. You must follow your dream.
And he was off. Sadly, they never met again.

August 15, 1947 was earmarked for the dawning of a new nation. The children all marched up to the town to witness the Indian flag being raised for the first time. Bond was 13 years old at that time. It was the height of the monsoons and there was a steady downpour. But that did not deter people. They poured out of their homes, marched into the streets, clambered onto rooftops and on trees. A sea of people under a sea of umbrellas. They all wanted to witness the unique moment in India's history. Amidst cheering and resounding applause, the Union Jack was lowered and the Indian flag hoisted. Little did Bond realise that two years later, as a school prefect, he would have the privilege of raising the Indian flag in the school grounds.

A few months later, whilst he was in a theatre watching the movie, *Blossoms in the Dust*, the film stopped running abruptly: Gandhiji had been shot. The nation was devastated. There was upheaval in the country once again. Just as the shining moon has dark patches, India's greatest moment of glory was scarred. However, slowly the fledgling country went about trying to find her feet once again.

1950. The last year of school was a watershed year for Bond. He became an angry young man, revolting against traditions and examinations. He rebelled against authority and the rules imposed on the students. His bête noire was Mr Fisher, the new headmaster. Perhaps, as Fisher did not have children of his own, he could not understand the tumultuous phase of adolescence. Unlike Mr Jones, the previous headmaster, Fisher was highly unapproachable. His wife, a plum pudding of a woman, indulged in gross favouritism.

Sadly, those whom she favoured a while ago soon became her target of hate and she would go all out to make trouble for them. Once, Bond let in a goal during a football match. She lashed out at him and called him a *doodhwala*. Angrily, he retaliated and called her a *doodhwali*. He was severely caned. Bond feels that perhaps the punishment was justified. She was the headmaster's wife after all, and he a mere student.

On another occasion, the quality of the food in school had fallen substantially. As Bond was their house captain, the boys lodged their complaints with him. When Fisher was on his rounds, Bond conveyed their message to him. He was promptly stripped of his captainship. It was restored later, but the reprimand seemed totally unfair to Bond. More trouble lay in store for Bond. He had always been weak in physics and this year it was Fisher who was taking the subject. During the half-yearly exams, in a rebellious mood, Bond submitted a blank answer sheet. Fisher, as you can guess, was livid. However, it wasn't just Bond who disliked him; he was generally unpopular with the students and also some of the faculty. A year after Bond had finished with school, he heard that Mr Fisher and his plum-pudding wife had had to leave the school in disgrace.

Bond graduated from school in 1950. Whilst all his friends were charting their future course—some going in for further studies, either in India or abroad, some deciding to join the Armed Forces, the Civil Services and a few joining their family business, Bond had decided that the future that he had envisaged for himself was to be independent. To do what he wanted. And what he wanted to do most was to write. "I am done with my studies. No college or further degrees for me," he declared. "Henceforth, my education will continue in second-hand bookstores!"

CHAPTER 11

The Room on the Roof

With his school years behind him, the future stretched tantalisingly before Bond—he was excited at the possibilities, but also afraid. Would he be able to succeed as a writer? Post-war, small town Dehra had limited job potential for most young men and more so for someone aspiring to be a writer. Also, there were virtually no publishing houses for English literature in India.

However, as that was what he really wanted to do, he sat in his little room on the roof and under the breeze of a small whirling fan, he plodded along...writing...sending out essays and short stories to all the prevailing magazines of those times and then waiting...waiting...waiting to hear from them.

His first story was published in one of the most prestigious magazines of those days, *The Illustrated Weekly*, and was titled 'My Calling'—a humourous piece on one of his school masters. He was paid fifty rupees for it. He was on his way to becoming an author! Soon, income started to trickle in. Pieces that were rejected by *The Weekly* or *The Sunday Statesman* would be sent off to *My Magazine of India* published from Chennai which paid five rupees per article or story. However, the income was not enough. He still needed his big break.

His family encouraged him to go to England as his aunt Emily who had migrated to Jersey offered to host him until he found his feet. Perhaps it was best to go to England, he thought. At least there he would be closer to the giants of literary publishing. But how was he to pay for his ticket? Fortunately for him, an insurance policy that Granny had taken out for him had matured and now he had some money in his hands. Not a lot, but just enough to pay for his fare and still have a little left to tide him over until he started to earn.

He planned to leave in November, still a few months away, and whilst he waited, he 'wandered lonely as a cloud', with his hands in his pockets, soaking in the sights and the sounds—the hoopoe foraging for insects in the ground, the dhobis swirling colourful clothes in the air, wild flowers sprouting from stone walls, muscled wrestlers resting under the peepul tree.

He was rootless and restless, more so because after Granny had passed away her house had been sold—the only constant home that he had known, one that had held many memories of his childhood.

Ever since his father had bought him his first diary, Bond regularly jotted down little anecdotes, interesting sights and also his feelings. These entries were a great source of inspiration for his stories. His first book, *The Room on the Roof*, also drew a lot of material inspiration from them. Here are a few excerpts from his diary describing the very first time he met Somi and gang, and the subsequent roller-coaster series of events.

'And then one day a ray of sunshine burst in through the door,' is how Bond described his first meeting with Somi. It was the start of a deep, fun-filled and caring friendship. One that resulted in months of sheer joy and happiness, years of nostalgia and an award-winning book.

February 28th

Haripal came to see me, and took me home to lunch. His house stood on the outskirts of the town where civilisation began to merge with the jungle. It was surrounded by an orchard of peach and plum trees which were covered with pink and white blossoms. A rich red, flowering bougainvillea creeper climbed the walls, and in front of the house were beds of poppies and marigolds. And there were bees and a swallow-tailed butterfly and sunshine.

"It is all Somi's garden,' said Haripal.

"Somi?"

"My brother. He's twelve years old."

His family was out, so we sat and talked, which is a very easy thing to do with Haripal.

At twelve o'clock a door burst open and a great happiness entered my life.

"This is Somi," said Haripal.

The boy smiled broadly and said: "Hello, Rusky. Hari says you'll do my English homework if I am your friend."

"Don't be funny, Somi. I never said that." Haripal's nose assumed a threatening attitude.

"Well, what if you did? I don't want Ruskin to do my homework, I want him to play with me." He sat on the arm of the chair, rested his chin on his hands, and looked at me steadily for a few moments. "Don't go."

"Where?" I asked.

"England. You must stay here. I like you."

"How can you like me without knowing me?"

"Oh, I know you now...will you like me?"

"Of course."

"Good, then we'll be best friends."

He had deep brown, beautiful, dreamy eyes, a broad forehead and muddy hands. The one I shook was warm and firm. His long hair was tied up in a bundle on his head. His features were fair complexioned but hard to notice under the mud that covered them. His feet were bare, his shorts torn.

All this was wonderful but the most wonderful of all was the laugh. There was a clear ring to it, and had an echo of its very own.

"Where have you been?" demanded Haripal. "And why aren't you wearing your turban?"

"I've been digging a hole at the back of the house and the turban is there too."

"Then go and get it!...Wait! Why are you digging a hole?"

"So as to bury the sweeper's dog...or do you want to bury it?"

"And now I'm sorry to say I have to go back to the animal hospital to bring the dog for burial. Bye!"

He departed as he had arrived; with a bang of the door.
Haripal said, "Isn't he chalak, a cunning rascal? Wait till you know him better...and you will know him better, for sure. Somi likes you, and once Somi likes a person he will never leave him."

And so the friendship began. Soon, they were something more than just friends, they were also his family—Somi, Haripal, Dipi, Chotu and Duljeet. They whizzed through by-lanes of Dehra on their bicycles, they shared their meals, they laughed, they played, they fought and they made up.

Bond had recently moved into a room that was built on the roof of a house. The roof was quite expansive and stretched into the welcoming arms of a tree. One day, when Somi was visiting Bond, they sat on the roof dangling their legs over the sides. "Ruskin, you should grow a garden on the roof."
Bond was thrilled. The idea of having a garden of his own, even if it was a rooftop one, was very exciting. "Will you help me if I make one?"
"Of course. I know where to get good seeds." And work began in right earnest. First, they surveyed the roof to see which parts were the sunniest. Then they planned the layout of the flower beds.

And so the friendship began. Soon, they were something more than just friends; they were also his family—Somi, Haripal, Dipi, Chotu and Duljeet. They whizzed through the by-lanes of Dehra on their bicycles, they shared their meals, they laughed, they played, they fought and they made up.

"Ruskin, you should grow a garden on the roof."

March 24th

Somi and I began work on the roof garden, and in honour of the occasion he played truant from school.

"Won't you get into trouble?" I asked.

"No, I was sent out of class. I did not wear my school uniform this morning, so they've sent me home to put it on."

"And aren't you going to do that?"

"No, I'll say that I tore the pants on the cycle."

We made an inspection of the waste garden in the compound and, finding a spot where the earth was dark and soft, began to dig—Somi, with a toy spade, and I with a poker. We had nothing else...no shovel, pickaxe, fork or spade.

But our problem was soon solved. Chotu suddenly appeared in our midst and in his arms was a dog.

It was a terrier of sorts, with a touch of dachshund and a retriever's tail. Its ears were mangy, its hair scruffy. But it had a face full of expression, eyes that were full of mischief.

"See, he will dig for you," said Chotu, going down on all fours himself and scraping at the hole we had made. "His name is Prickly Heat...rats, rats!"

The mongrel yelped joyously and dashed at the hole, pawing, scraping, scooping up mounds of mud. Chotu manned a bucket, Somi a watering can, and I an old flowerpot, and together we filled them with earth.

We climbed the steps to the roof in relays, Prickly Heat running around us and barking furiously, his tail revolving in a complete circle... We had laid out two beds before the sun set. Our hands were muddy, scratched and blistered.

"That's all for today," announced Somi, "but I'll plant the first seeds before I go." He sprinkled a few over one of the beds.

"What were they?" I asked.

"Pumpkins."

I was indignant. "But I don't want vegetables, I want flowers."

"You can have flowers... What's wrong with vegetables? We can eat them."

"Yes, but how will it look, marigolds and pumpkins all mixed up!"

"Very nice," said Chotu. "Very nice."

The trees became very noisy as Somi and Chotu were about to go. "The birds are talking about us," said Somi. "They also think we are mad."

After they had all left, Bond entered his room. What a mess there was! The water from the watering can had spilled all over, blobs of mud covered the floor and Prickly Heat had snuggled up under his sheets—muddy paws and all.

Soon those sunny carefree fun-filled days came to an end. It was time for Bond to leave. On a gray wintry morning, he left for the train station accompanied by his friends and a deep sadness.

They stood outside his compartment. No one spoke. Words were not necessary.

Dong! Dong! The gong sounded. Chotu clung to Bond. Pheww! The whistle blew. Haripal and Kishen shook his hand. Chug, chug, chug! The train started to pull out. Dul hugged him.

Bond jumped into the moving train. With tears running down his cheeks, Somi ran alongside Bond's compartment for as long as he could. "Goodbye, Ruskin," he shouted. "Do not forget how to laugh!"

CHAPTER 12

Towards Greener Pastures

Almost a decade after the family had left the gentle waves of the shores of Jamnagar, Bond was once again on the waters of the Arabian Sea. This time he was heading for England in search of greener pastures. Before the days of air travel, big passenger liners used to ply on the ocean. Bond set sail from Bombay in the *S.S. Strathnaver*, for a fifteen-day journey that passed through colourful ports along the Suez Canal and the Red Sea before the ship docked in a port near London. From there he boarded a ferry to Jersey, where he was to live for two years.

By the time he reached his aunt's house in St. Helier's, the capital city of Jersey, he had only about three or four pounds of his travel money left, and worse, he was sick. He had picked up a bug in Bombay and was laid low with jaundice for almost two weeks. As soon as he was back on his feet, he started looking for a job.

At first, he did a round of all the solicitors' offices thinking that perhaps they would have some clerical work for him. But owing to his young age (he was only seventeen years old at that time) and his lack of experience, he did not meet with any success. Soon he was down to his last pound. Out of sheer desperation he took up a job at a grocery store—Le Riche's—where he had to sit all day on a high chair, in front of a high desk, and prepare long boring bills.

The store was located near the pier—a twenty-minute walk from home. In the beginning, Bond enjoyed the walk over the gale-swept hill and across the promenade. However, as winter approached, the icy cold winds cut right through his tweed jacket—he did not have an overcoat—and chilled his very bones. To add to his woes, the boss was always looking over the employees' shoulders to make sure they worked non-stop. "Stop dreaming, Bond, and get on with those bills," he would shout. Work was paramount: Bond was shocked that even when King George VI died, unlike India, where everything shuts down when an important political leader dies, they merely observed a few minutes' silence as a mark of respect and then—back to work!

Within three months, the tedious work, the long hours, the meagre pay and the uninteresting fellow workers got to him. He could not take it anymore and he quit the job.

Luckily, he found an opening in a newly-opened branch of a famous travel agency, Thomas Cook. His new boss, a Miss Manning, was a chain smoker and did not remove her cigarette even whilst talking on the phone! All day long, she would go puff-puff-puff. Sometimes, she would take off with her boyfriend, leaving Bond in charge of making the bookings.

Jersey was very colour-conscious in those days and did not accept any dark-skinned tourists from the African, Asian or even the American continents. Once, whilst she was away, he committed an unforgivable sin: he booked a group of Brazilian samba dancers into a whites-only hotel. That spelt the end of his career at the travel agency. He was fired.

His next job was far better than the previous two. It was in a public health department. His fellow clerks were definitely more friendly than those in his previous jobs and one of them, Mr Bromley, was a sympathetic soul. He was an avid reader and had even tried his hand at writing. Having failed at which, he admired Bond's dogged determination to be a writer.

Once, he spotted Bond standing in front of a shop window gazing wistfully at a portable typewriter. Bond had nearly finished writing his manuscript (by hand, as he does even today) and needed to type it out before sending it to various publishers.
SALE
•TYPEWRITERS•
Looking to buy the typewriter, lad?
I wish I could. Sadly, I can't afford it. I have been able to save only six pounds so far, and this beauty costs nineteen! I guess I'll just have to hire one.
I tell you what, chappie, give me your six pounds and I'll put in the balance for you.
Bond was stunned at his generosity. He started to protest.
Publishers do not appreciate a messy-looking manuscript. If you really want to be published, my boy, you must send out a neat-looking one. Don't worry, you can pay me back one pound per week from your salary.

But all was not smooth sailing. Whilst staying in his aunt's house, he found that although they were Anglo-Indian, they desperately tried to shake off their Indian roots. Sometimes they would even ridicule his Indian connection—his friends, his accent and his yearning for India. Upset at their attitude, he poured his anger and resentment onto paper. One day his uncle found the diary in which he had entered the derogatory remarks about the family and their superiority complex. They were furious and accused him of being ungrateful, he in turn accused them of prying. Angry words followed. After a couple of days, matters settled down, but the pot was still simmering and although no more was said, the silence was ominous.

Highly disturbed, Bond went for a walk on the seafront. The tide was in, the winds swirled around crazily, whipping up giant waves that crashed into the sea wall. The gale-force winds and the salt spray beating down upon him were both exhilarating and liberating. At that moment he could see his path ahead very clearly.

He shouted above the sound of the roaring wind, "I will be a writer, I am going to write, and no one can stop me!" He decided to relocate to London where he would be his own master—completely independent. Not only that, he would also be closer to the big publishing houses where perhaps he would stand a better chance of fulfilling his dream of becoming a published writer.

So, armed solely with determination and twelve pounds saved from his salary, he boarded the cross-channel ferry, carrying a battered old suitcase stuffed with his clothes in one hand and his precious typewriter in the other. Soon he was in London.

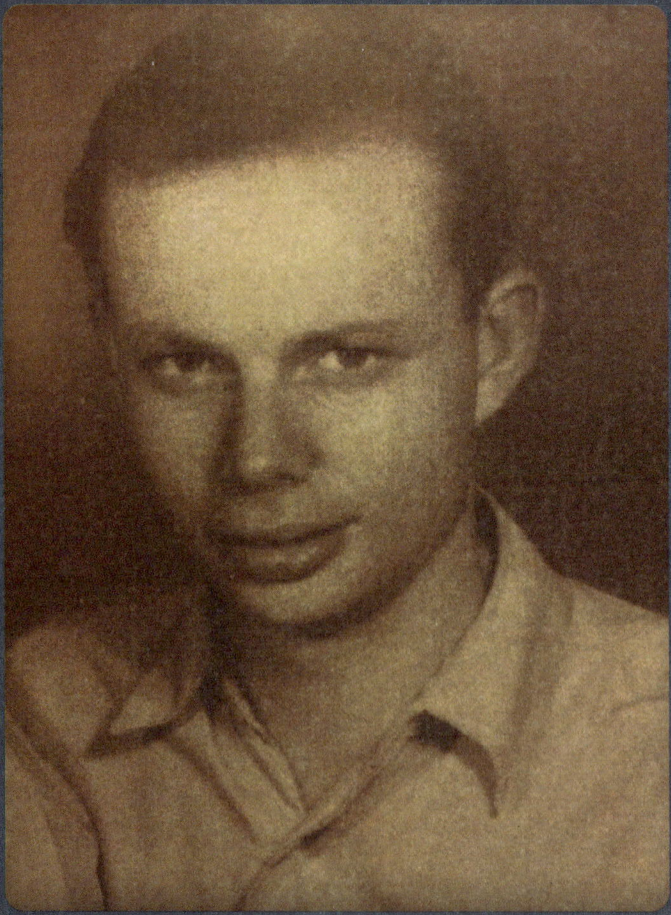

CHAPTER 13

London

London! A city bustling with life. Home to iconic buildings, such as the Buckingham Palace, Big Ben and the Tower of London; museums that housed rich collections from all over the world; well-stocked libraries; resplendent theatres that staged musicals and luxurious cinemas. Dotting the landscape were leafy green parks, gardens and boulevards. Bond longed to saunter through the secret lanes, the docks and the backwaters that used to be the haunts of the great literary characters who had captured his imagination all through his growing years—Dickens, P. G. Wodehouse, Shakespeare, J. M. Barrie and others. However, as he had only 12 pounds in his pocket, what he needed to do right away was to find a cheap place to live in, and a job!

He wandered around until he found the cheapest possible place—a student's hostel. The next day, he went to the employment exchange to find a job. By this time he had changed so many that he did not care what the job was, as long as it paid him enough to pay for his room and board and left him with time to write.

He found a job at Photax, a photographic store. Unfortunately, a couple of months later, his right eye started to bother him. At first, it began to cloud over and soon his vision was partially affected.

He was admitted into a hospital where it was detected that he had Eales Disease, a rare condition that could have been aggravated owing to his poor diet. Luckily it was curable and after spending almost a month in the Hampstead General Hospital he was discharged. Not only did his eye get better, but because of the nourishing diet, he was in a far better shape than he had gone in—literally!

After spending a month in the hospital, getting back to real life was a bit hard. He went back to Photax where he had to add up figures in bulky ledgers all day long. It was no fun and neither were his colleagues. And as for the poky little bedsitter rooms that he lived in, the less spoken about them, the better. They either smelled or had bed bugs or had plaster peeling off the walls—in short, they were gloomy, depressing and unbearable. By the end of the two years that he spent in London, he had lived in many bedsitters across the city—Hampstead, Belsize Park, Swiss Cottage, Tooting.

To add to his woes, London was also a very challenging place for someone so far away from home. It was very difficult to shed the all-engulfing loneliness.

One never even met the other lodgers unless they came in to complain that the radio was too loud. Either one strolled aimlessly in the streets, or went to the nearest snack bar or restaurant or, sat in a cinema or, took a bath in the public bathing rooms where for 2 shillings and 6 pence one was given a clean towel, a small cake of soap and a tub of piping hot water. His only consolation was that there were thousands of others living just like him—sans money, sans friends, sans life.

And then he met Vu-Phuong, a girl from Vietnam. She came in as a ray of sunshine into his life. They went on long walks together on Primrose Hill. They ate their meals together after which she would tell him his fortune by reading the patterns that formed after the tea was drunk. She even predicted that someday he would be famous.

Bond fell head over heels in love with her. He proposed to her and wanted to marry her as soon as possible. However, she told him that as hers was a conservative family, she would have to seek her parents' permission and would do so when she went to Vietnam. When she left, Bond was heartbroken. He framed a picture of her and kept it on his desk and waited and waited and waited. But it was in vain. She did not return, and worse, she did not even write.

They went for long walks.
They ate their meals together after which she would tell him his fortune by reading the patterns that formed after the tea was drunk.
Oh! It says that you're going to be famous someday!
When she left for Vietnam, Bond was heartbroken.
He framed a picture of her and kept it on his desk and waited and waited and waited...

Two lonely years had gone by in London. By now Bond was quite homesick.

He yearned for:
Bright blue skies...
Brown-skinned kids...
Mango blossoms...
Girls in pink dupattas...
Swirls of dust...
Water lilies in village ponds...
Sharp flavours of pungent food...
Steaming hot cups of chai...
Fragrance of the earth after the first rains...
His friends...
His life...
His home...India

And although his ancestors were English and although English was the language he was most comfortable with and although England was the cradle of great literature, he realised that it was not for him. He wanted to be where his heart was—and his heart was very much in India.

Bond plunged himself with even greater vigour into his book. *The Room on the Roof* had been accepted by Andre Deutsch's publishing firm. But they wanted him to make certain changes and he spent most nights working on it.

It was in its third edit by now. First, the publishers had suggested that he 'fill' it out and then he was told that it was too wordy and that he needed to prune it down. Also, initially the book was written in the form of a journal which was changed into a first person narrative and finally ended up being written in the third person. However, in spite of the many changes, the essence of the story stayed the same and so did the title, *The Room on the Roof*.

Andre Deutsch and his sub-editor Diana Athill were very positive about it. Diana spent a lot of time with Bond, talking about the book and other things. They became good friends. Sensing his loneliness and also appreciative of his spirit and determination, she took him under her wing, cooking occasional meals for him and accompanying him on long walks.

However, months passed by and there was no commitment from the firm. Finally, in August of 1953, Bond shot Mr Deutsch a long politely worded letter demanding to know where he stood. Bond expressed his frustration at being made to wait interminably to get a final nod to his book.

This is what he wrote:

"…However, August 1953 is a long way from December 1952, when I first came to you, and though I am aware and appreciative of the many ways in which I have benefitted from my perseverance with your firm, I now feel that I have been 'on the rack' long enough and that I deserve a final decision. I would like to stress my appreciation of the fact that you are busy people, and that whilst I have only one book to worry about, you have scores; and I also appreciate the fact that I am very young and can therefore be made to wait. Indeed, I am only too glad to wait, provided I know there is something to wait for…

I have not wanted to write this letter, because I have not wanted to hurry you, because to hurry you might have been to spoil my chances. But I must risk offending you by asking that you please give me your final decision by the end of the month.

If this letter has already convinced you of my utter unsuitability for the role of one of your authors, I would appreciate the return of my MS of The Room on the Roof. I do not ask for any favours. I want no friendship. I only want business.

If you have incurred any expenses on my behalf, such as the payment of fees to readers, please do send me a bill for the same."

The letter worked! Perhaps because of the very mature approach taken by the author, perhaps it was going to be sent anyway, perhaps because they were reluctant to part with the manuscript. Whatever the reason, Bond received a cheque for fifty pounds, the standard royalty in those days. He was overjoyed. With this money plus his savings plus a small amount received from BBC for a story he had submitted, he now had enough money to buy himself a ticket on the Polish liner, *S. S. Batory*, and would soon be homeward bound.

In March 1954, the icy cold waters of the English Channel were slowly left behind. Soon they were in the warmer waters of the Mediterranean and a couple of days later in the even warmer waters of the Red Sea. With the warmth of the sun on his body, a warm balmy breeze on his face and an even warmer feeling in his heart, Bond stood on the deck awaiting the final docking of the ship in the port of his eagerly awaited destination on the Arabian Sea—India.

CHAPTER 14

Homeward Bound!

The journey back home on the *S. S. Batory* turned out to be quite dramatic!

One night, the passengers were suddenly jolted out of their sleep with the wild clanging of the ship's alarm bells. Startled, everyone jumped out of their bunks and rushed onto the deck, still clothed in their pajamas. Their first thought was that the ship was sinking. They ran helter-skelter like headless chicken. No one knew what to do but at the same time they all felt as though they had to do something. Loud shrieks, screams and shouts shattered the stillness of the night sky. Help! Abandon ship! Man overboard! and even 'Women and children first!' (Although there were no women and children anywhere around). The hysteria abated and sanity returned when they found out that it was not their lives that were in danger but that of a tipsy passenger who had fallen overboard. The passengers heaved a sigh of relief and one by one crept back into their bunks. The crew lowered the lifeboats into the dark, rolling waters to search for the missing passenger.
Was he found? Bond never got to know.

The saga of the *Batory* was far from over. When they finally docked at port, a fire broke out in the hold of the ship. Many people lost their luggage, but luckily for Bond, he had kept his precious typewriter and his suitcases of clothes and gifts by his side all through the journey. He was afraid of losing them, for he knew that if ever they were lost, he would not be able to buy clothes, and definitely not a typewriter for a long time to come.

When he arrived at Delhi railway station he was surprised to see his stepfather waiting to receive him. It marked the beginning of a more mature relationship. Whilst on the train to Dehradun, Hari informed Bond that he had a job offer in Delhi and would soon be leaving with the family. Bond was welcome to join them. An offer Bond promptly refused.

The train was slowly pulling into the tiny Dehra station. Waiting for him on the platform was his friend, Dipi. With a whoop of joy, Bond jumped off the train and hugged his friend. He quickly piled his bags and typewriter into his stepfather's car, hopped onto the crossbar of Dipi's cycle and off they sailed, whizzing past the familiar sights of the town, just as in the good old days!

Bond was twenty-one years old and a new phase of his life was about to begin.

After the first few days of sheer joy at being back on hallowed ground, Bond took stock of his finances. From the fifty pounds advance that he had received from Andre Deutsch, he barely had eight hundred rupees left.

His family was moving to Delhi and that meant that he would have to now bear the cost of boarding and lodging.

Luckily for him, Bibiji, his stepfather's ex-wife, offered him a room above her small grocery store. Along with it came a balcony from where he could sit and watch the world go by. The furniture, though sparse, was enough for his needs. It had a bed and a 'desk' which was actually a large dining table and on the desk were his papers weighed down by a smooth well-rounded stone from the river. On the desk sat a kerosene lamp that Bond had purchased, as Bibiji's electricity supply had been disconnected for not having paid her electricity bill for months on end.

On the desk also sat two photo frames—one of his father and the other of Vu-Phuong, the Vietnamese girl to whom he had proposed marriage. However, as the months passed by and he did not hear from her, with a heavy heart, he put it away in an album of memories.

Bond was very comfortable in Bibiji's house. The best part of staying there was that he kick-started his day with a hearty breakfast of paranthas stuffed with either aloo or mooli, accompanied by a deliciously spicy shalgam (turnip) pickle. After this sumptuous breakfast, Bond would sit at his desk and write; his target being a thousand words a day which he usually achieved in a couple of hours. He usually wrote in longhand and once he was happy with the content, he would type out the fair copy, making some minor revisions as he went along. Soon, his works started appearing regularly in magazines—both in India and in England—and although they did not make him rich or famous, he earned enough to get by.

Lunch was usually a simple affair taken at some dhaba. If he stuck to basic fare, such as dal, rice and some vegetable, he could eat for as little as three rupees! In the evening he would generally stroll to the clock tower to hang out with friends and munch on the delicious tikkias or kebabs sold by street vendors. Once, he even took up a challenge thrown at him by a friend and ate thirty tikkias in one go—with results that are not very difficult to predict!

As night set in, Bond would return 'home', light the kerosene lantern and under its flickering light, jot down some thoughts, ideas for his stories, or write a letter or two.

One day, his London publisher, Andre Deutsch, informed him that he had sold the German rights to his novel, *The Room on the Roof*. The royalty was pretty substantial and this enabled him to continue to write what he wanted, where he wanted.

And then there was some more good news. *The Room on the Roof* appeared in a serialised version in the most popular magazine of the time—*The Illustrated Weekly of India.*

Clutching the magazines that he had purchased from the vendor, he reached home and as he re-read the story for the umpteenth time, he let out a deep satisfied sigh. *The Room on the Roof* was finally in print and it was time to celebrate! That evening, Bond got together with his friends to celebrate the momentous event.

Happily tired, he returned home late evening, and then it was back to work. He trimmed the wick of the kerosene lamp, sat down at his desk, picked up his pen, pulled out a fresh sheet of paper and began to write.

And more than sixty years and a hundred and sixty books later the thespian still writes on...

...And lives happily ever after...

...with his (adopted) family

Around the year 1970, Prem Singh, then a young boy, all of sixteen years, walked into Bond's life. He was tall, earnest and had a presence that appealed to him. He took an instant liking to the young lad. At that time, Prem's uncle was working with Bond, and so he helped Prem find a job elsewhere. A couple of years later, the uncle left for greener pastures and Prem appeared once again at his door.

"Will you work for me now?" asked Bond.
"For as long as you wish."
"For as long as the gods wish," replied Bond. The gods were apparently delighted at the arrangement as Prem was hard-working and sincere and they began to share a warm comradeship.

A year later, Prem married Chandra, a good-looking girl from his village. They have three children—two sons, Rakesh and Mukesh, and a daughter, Savitri.

Bond enjoyed watching the family grow. His house was filled with the happy patter of feet, joyous laughter and childhood prattle. He also participated in caring for the young boys, often taking them to school, telling them stories and even better, writing several stories for them! 'The Cherry Tree' was written for Rakesh and 'Earthquake' and others for all of them.

When they were older, Rakesh and Mukesh found for themselves two sisters as brides—Beena and Benita. Between them they have given Prem and Bond four lovely grandsons and two grand-daughters. Savitri, the youngest, nicknamed Dolly is also married and has three children. Over the years, they moved houses several times before finally settling into their current home, Ivy Cottage. Today, Rakesh, his wife Beena and their three children, Siddharth, Gautam and Shrishti live with him in Ivy Cottage, whilst Prem, Mukesh and his children, Atish and Vaishnavi, live down the road.

Thus, in spite of never having married, Bond today is very much a family man surrounded by love. And to this day he is still a great goal-keeper, only now he does not merely guard his goalpost as he did during his school years, but goes all out to protect his loved ones, his turf and his way of life.

...with sweet memories
...of running away from home

Once, it so happened that in a rebellious mood young Ruskin decided to run away from home.
It was late January and Dehra was in the grip of a cold wave. Having taken nothing with him, he was quite unprepared for the weather and wondered where he could spend the night.

His options were:

• *In the maidan*. He quickly ruled that out as he would have probably frozen to death.

• *At the railway station.* Several vagrants usually snuggled into their woollen blankets on the benches. Bond did not have a blanket of his own and even the thought of sharing theirs—perhaps infested with bedbugs and lice, made him feel itchy and scratchy all over!

• *At a friend's house.* His friend Bhim had once firmly declared himself to be his buddy and well-wisher. Now that was a possible option.

Sure enough, Bhim lived up to his promise and willingly offered to share his room with Bond.
After dinner that night, they huddled in their blankets as Bhim tried to chart out Bond's survival strategy.
"Do you have any money?"
"Uh-uh," responded Bond glumly.
"Then you have to sell some of your possessions."
"Don't have any."
"Oh-oh. That's not good. Not good at all." Suddenly he exclaimed, "Hey! What about your books? The ones you won as prizes. They belong to you, don't they?"
"Y-yes."
"That's it! Tomorrow we'll go to Universal Book Store and sell them!"

Next morning, Bond quietly sneaked into his house and with a heavy heart gathered his prized books—*The Complete Shakespeare* (the Hailey Literature Prize), *Pearson's Biography of Dickens* (the Anderson Essay Prize) and several others and sold them. Bhim took charge of the money. After deducting his commission, he handed the balance amount to Bond.

Sadly, the money (approximately one hundred rupees) disappeared like mist in the early morning sunshine. A couple of days later, having had enough of being a runaway, Bond returned home.

"What's for lunch?" he cheerily called out to no one in particular and sat down to eat!

...of Uncle Ken

Uncle Ken was an indolent and lazy person. Having four doting aunts, he usually flitted from one home to another, living with each for about three months and thus got away from the irksome issue of having to earn a living.

There was usually a healthy animosity between Bond and Uncle Ken. On one occasion, Granny had made some roast duck for dinner and Uncle Ken selfishly transferred two large helpings and also most of the stuffing onto his plate. To get even, Ruskin wickedly emptied out most of the applesauce onto his own plate. As Ruskin loved the stuffing and Uncle Ken the applesauce, it was tit for tat!

On another occasion, Ruskin was playing with his marbles in the garden whilst Uncle Ken stretched out under the red silk-cotton tree and started to smoke a cigar. What he did not realise was that a huge beehive was suspended from a branch of the tree directly above him. Disturbed by the fumes, the wild bees charged at him angrily. With great presence of mind, Uncle Ken dashed indoors and leapt into a tub of cold water, but not before the bees had successfully expressed their displeasure. Covered with stings, poor Uncle Ken had to stay in bed for the next few days, much to the delight of little Ruskin!

...with his books

All his life, Bond has been an avid reader. His house is stocked with books; well thumbed books that he had read, loved and enjoyed over the years. A few of his favourite authors being Charles Dickens, Emily Bronte, W. Somerset Maugham, Hugh Walpole, Rabindranath Tagore, R. L. Stevenson and J. M. Barrie.

Everywhere you look in his house you see books—on shelves, in cupboards, on tables and even on the stairs all the way up to the ceiling! In fact, the books that he had read all through his growing years inspired him to be a writer.

"I am a fortunate person to be able to make a living by doing what I love most—writing," says Bond. And he has never stopped writing. "We cannot prevent sorrow and pain and tragedy. And yet when we look around us, we realise that there are so many lovely things to see, there is so much to do, so much fun to be had, and so many charming and interesting people to meet... How can my pen ever run dry?"

Best of all, he can write anywhere. All he needs is a sharp pencil and some paper to get his stories to start to unfold. Often, he will lie on the grass and write for hours. For Bond writing is the simplest and greatest pleasure in the world, hence, a nine-to-five job was definitely not for him, although it would have given him a steady income and perhaps, retirement benefits.

The sincerity, simplicity and passion with which he writes has enchanted readers for decades. Book after book has followed. So much so, that if one were to purchase all his books, one would need several bookshelves to be able to stock them all!
And the moving finger writes on...

...his thoughts

Bond is a quiet introspective person who loves to observe nature, people and even himself. From these deep pools of calm and quietude arise many inspiring thoughts.
"As a boy, reading was my religion. It helped me to discover my soul. Later, writing helped me to record its journey."

- May you have the wisdom to be simple, and the humour to be happy.
- Experience: the knowledge that enables you to recognise a mistake when you make it the second time.
- Be proud of what you are and what you've done. But be proud within.
- Never despair. But if you do, work on in despair.
- A great book is a friend that never lets you down.
- To be true to oneself is to be true to others.
- Life isn't always pleasant, but I find it's possible to shut out the darker recollections and dwell instead on life's happier moments.
- Hold onto your dreams,
  Do not let them die.
  We are lame without them—
  Birds that cannot fly.

...surrounded by nature

revelling in the ever-changing facets of nature—be it the weather or flora and fauna, Bond pens his observations:

...about the night

"Here in Landour, on the first range of the Himalayas, I have grown accustomed to the night's brightness—moonlight, starlight, lamplight, firelight! Even fireflies and glowworms light up the darkness.
Walking home at midnight can be quite eventful, but in a different sort of way. One is conscious all the time of the silent life in the surrounding trees and bushes. I have smelt a leopard without seeing it. I have seen jackals on the prowl. I have watched foxes dance in the moonlight. I have seen flying squirrels flit from one treetop to another. I have observed pine martens on their nocturnal journeys, and listened to the calls of the nightjars and owls and other birds who live by night."

...about snakes

"Now that the rains are here, the occasional snake, flooded out of its home, makes its appearance on the road or hillside. Most of the snakes are pretty harmless, carrying only enough venom to paralyse their natural prey; which consist of frogs, rats, earthworms, small birds and smaller snakes."

...about insects

"Our insect musicians are roused to the greatest activity during the monsoons. At dusk the air seems to tinkle and murmur to their music. To the shrilling of the grasshoppers is added the staccato notes of the crickets, while in the grass and on the trees myriads of lesser artistes are producing a variety of sounds."

...about flowers

"And which flower is most redolent of India, of the heat and light and colour of India? Not for me the lotus or the water-lily, but the single marigold, fresh, dew-drenched, kissed by the morning sun."

...about trees

"The oaks (these are not English oaks) are rather stunted and untidy, but they are hospitable to birds and insects. The peepul, with its beautiful heart-shaped leaf catches the breeze and flutters even on the stillest of days. The deodar is the most noble tree of the Himalayas. It has dignity, grace and strength. Watch it shrug the snow off its shoulders with gentle disdain and you will get an idea of its dignity. Watch it catch the wind and make it sing, sadly and softly, in its slim green branches, and you will get an idea of its divinity. It is not as fragrant as the pine, but it makes sweeter music." Bond even wrote a poem dedicated to trees:

They know me well, these trees:
Oak and walnut, spruce and pine,
They know my face in the window,
They know me for a dreamer of dreams,
A world-loser, one of them.
They watch me while I watch them grow.
I listen to their whisperings,
Their own mysterious diction;
And bow my head before their arms
And ask for benediction.

...winning awards

In 1957, his very first book, *The Room on the Roof*, hit the bullseye and won him the John Llewellyn Rhys Prize awarded to a British Commonwealth writer under 30 years of age.

He received the Sahitya Akademi Award for English writing in India for *Our Trees Still Grow in Dehra* in 1992.
The Padma Shri was conferred upon him in 1999, followed by one of the most prestigious civil awards in India—the Padma Bhushan in 2014.

...accolades

Many of his books have been included as part of the school curriculum all over India. *The Room on the Roof*, *The Night Train at Deoli* and *Our Trees Still Grow in Dehra*, among others.
Some of his works have even been adapted into film. His novella, *The Flight of Pigeons* was adapted into a Shyam Benegal film, *Junoon*, *The Blue Umbrella* was filmed by Vishal Bharadwaj, as was *Susanna's Seven Husbands (Saat Khoon Maaf)*.

...and adulation

"Thank you for making my childhood so beautiful. I've grown up with your stories." *Your biggest fan, Aditi Holmes*

"You have been an inspiration, not only for me to take up writing, but also to take the time to stop and appreciate the small joys, the little gifts of nature and the pure joy of friendship!" *Kay*

"You have been the constant companion in all ups and downs of my life. You inspire me, you motivate me and you teach me how to live life to the fullest." *Rakhi Sharma*

"Sir, know this that you have given countless people thousands of reasons to smile and look at themselves, and life, in a far more positive light." *Ritesh Khandelwal*

"Your books, for me symbolise hope and light. I'm not very good with words, and what I have written might probably look like a child's attempt at being philosophic. But I just want you to know that your books mean the world to me and more." *Amna Khan*

"Dear Mr. Bond, you are the one person who gave our imagination wings and through your words we visited worlds we were never aware of." *Chikirsha*

"Thank you for all the stories that have helped so many of us grow into wonderful humans and have fuelled our imaginations!" *Nandini Sharma*

ACKNOWLEDGEMENTS

Through all my tumultuous growing years, I always found succour in books, especially biographies. They taught me many important lessons—such as—nothing is really impossible if one sets one's heart and mind to achieving one's goal.

I never imagined that someday I would be writing the biographies of a few of the great lives of India. I am very grateful to Tina Narang for giving me this opportunity to write about A. P. J. Abdul Kalam, one of India's most beloved leaders, and also the biography of Ruskin Bond—a writer whose works have captured the hearts of millions of children across India.

Thank you, Tina, for trusting me to pen the lives of these iconic personalities. It has been a daunting task, but at the same time it has been a great learning and humbling experience.

I would also like to thank Rayika Sen for her delightful illustrations. They have lent a magical aura to the look of the book.

Most of all, my humble gratitude to the great writer himself for not only sparing two days in which to enable me to interview him and quiz him about his life, but also for reading my manuscript and giving some very valuable suggestions.

Dear readers, thank you for picking up this book. Whilst it is an easy read—simple and anecdotal in style—it carries within its pages great messages of courage, fortitude and the 'Never say Die' spirit of the great man himself—Ruskin Bond.

MORE SCHOLASTIC BIOGRAPHIES

Great Lives
Verghese Kurien
The Milkman of India
Rohini Chowdhury
Illustrations: Dhruva Rao

ISBN: 9789351032779
Pages: 132

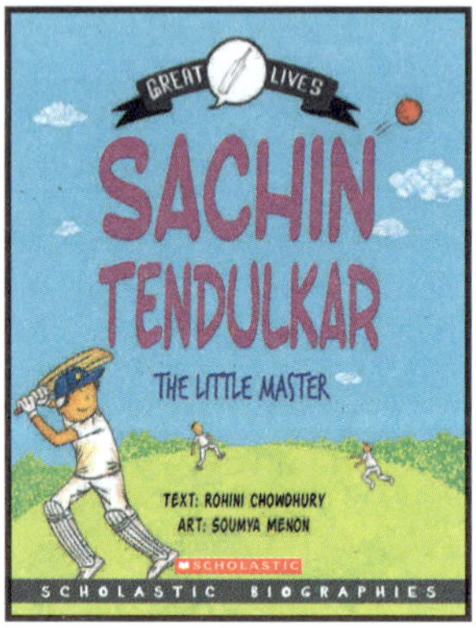

Great Lives
Sachin Tendulkar
The Little Master
Rohini Chowdhury
Illustrations: Soumya Menon

ISBN: 9789351038627
Pages: 108

Great Lives
Mohandas Karamchand Gandhi
Aditi De
Illustrations: Pooja Pottenkulam

ISBN: 9789351039938
Pages: 148

Great Lives
A. P. J. Abdul Kalam
The People's President
Shamim Padamsee
Illustrations: Lavanya Karthik

ISBN: 9788184779745
Pages: 104